W9-AYR-734

RI

HUNTING

OUTDOOR ADVENTURES

DAVID ARMENTROUT

The Rourke Press, Inc.
Vero Beach, Florida 32964

8486003

© 1998 The Rourke Press, Inc.

All rights reserved. No part of this book may be reproduced or utilized in any form or by any means, electronic or mechanical including photocopying, recording, or by any information storage and retrieval system without permission in writing from the publisher.

David Armentrout specializes in nonfiction writing and has had several book series published for primary schools. He resides in Cincinnati with his wife and two children.

PHOTO CREDITS
© Dave Henderson: cover; © East Coast Studios: page 9; © Dusty Willison/International Stock: page 4; © Ron Bielefeld: page 6; © Buddy Mays/International Stock: page 7; © Corel Corporation: pages 10,12, 21; © Scott WM Hanrahan/International Stock: page 18; © U.S. Fish and Wlldlife Service: page 19; © Sockman/International Stock: page 22 © Craig Bihrle: pages 13, 15, 16

EDITORIAL SERVICES:
Penworthy Learning Systems

Library of Congress Cataloging-in-Publication Data

Armentrout, David, 1962-
   Hunting / David Armentrout.
    p. cm. — (Outdoor adventures)
   Includes index.
   Summary: Describes different methods of hunting, hunting safety and laws, and wildlife management.
   ISBN 1-57103-206-1
   1. Hunting—Juvenile literature. [1. Hunting.] I. Title II. Series:
Armentrout, David. 1962- Outdoor adventures.
SK35.5.A75 1998
799.2—dc21   98–4290
                                                 CIP
                                                 AC

Printed in the USA

TABLE OF CONTENTS

HUNTING

People have always hunted animals. Before there were farms and grocery stores, people had to hunt or grow everything they ate. Hunting provided food to eat, fur and leather for clothing, and **hides** (HYDZ) for shelter.

Today some people still hunt for food. Others hunt and kill animals to stuff and display. Many people object to this type of hunting.

Shooting a gun takes training and practice.

WHAT PEOPLE HUNT

Many kinds of animals are taken by hunters. Bears, elks, and moose are called big game. Squirrels and rabbits are small game. Geese and ducks are waterfowl. Turkeys, grouse (GROUS), and pheasants (FEZ unts) are called upland game birds.

Two waterfowls land to join the flock.

A male deer can be recognized by its antlers.

Deer are big game and are hunted in every state. Most hunters prefer hunting male deer, called bucks, because they are big and supply a lot of meat. Bucks can also have a rack of **antlers** (ANT lurz) that hunters keep as a prize.

GUNS AND "AMMO"

Many kinds of guns are used for hunting. The type of gun you choose depends on the kind of animal you will hunt.

A shotgun has a long, fat barrel. It shoots shells. A shotgun shell is filled with little balls, called buckshot. The buckshot spreads out after the gun is fired. This makes it easier to hit your target. Hunters use shotguns when hunting small game or waterfowl.

A **rifle** (RY ful) has a thin barrel that shoots a lead bullet. Hunters use rifles to shoot big game.

Rifles often have a scope to help hunters see the target.

BOW HUNTING

Long ago, Native Americans hunted with bows and arrows. Arrows can be shot from a distance. Hunters could shoot an animal without getting too close.

Bow hunting is still popular with many hunters. Big and small game can be hunted with a bow and arrow.

Hunting with a bow and arrow takes special skills. There are bow hunting clubs and magazines for bow hunters. People who shoot with a bow and arrow are called **archers** (AHR cherz).

Shooting a bow requires a very steady hand.

HUNTING WITH DOGS

Dogs have a great sense of smell and are natural hunters. Some kinds of dogs are trained to help hunters find their **prey** (PRAY).

Some dogs are good at bringing back waterfowl to a hunter.

Hunting requires patience to sit and wait for an animal.

Dogs are often used to hunt game birds. Dogs locate the birds with their keen sense of smell. The birds are then flushed, or scared, from their hiding place. After the hunter shoots a bird, the dog brings it to its master.

In most states it is **illegal** (eh LEE gul), or against the law, to use dogs to hunt big game. Dogs give an unfair advantage to hunters.

HUNTING SAFELY

The use of guns and bows and arrows is risky. It is important to take a gun safety course to learn as much as you can about the gun you will be using. Good hunters spend as much time as they can at a **target** (TAHR git) range where they practice shooting.

All hunters should take a safety course before going on their first hunt. Hunting clubs and state offices offer courses before the start of each hunting season. Remember that safety comes first when hunting.

This boy is getting proper adult instructions for using his gun.

KNOW THE RULES

There are laws that hunters must follow. Some laws protect animals and some laws protect people.

Most hunters need a license to hunt. Every state has its own **game laws** (GAYM LAWZ). Check with the Fish and Game Department to find out what the laws are in your state.

National game laws also must be obeyed. The U.S. Fish and Wildlife Service is the government office in charge of these laws.

Experienced hunters often teach kids how to hunt.

WILDLIFE MANAGEMENT

Predators (PRED uh turz), like wolves and mountain lions, help keep the animal population in balance by killing off the old and weak.

Not as many predators are around today as there used to be. Without predators, some animal populations grow too fast.

Grizzly bears no longer help control animal population.

A U.S. Fish and Wildlife officer keeps track of what hunters kill.

Soon there are too many animals and not enough food for them to eat. Many of these animals may starve to death.

Hunting may seem cruel, but it is often the only way to control the number of animals. The animals that have been killed provide food for people, and the animals that remain may grow strong and healthy.

ILLEGAL HUNTING

Hunting is a sport, but it is also a way of life for many people. Legal hunting does not wipe out animal populations. It may be good for the **environment** (en VY run ment).

Illegal hunting, or **poaching** (POCH ing), can be harmful to nature. Two kinds of poaching are common. One kind occurs when a hunter takes animals at a time when hunting is not allowed. Another kind occurs when a hunter kills an animal that the game laws say cannot be hunted.

Poachers who are caught may be put in jail and made to pay large fines.

The bald eagle, protected by U.S. law, is often a target for poachers.

GLOSSARY

antlers (ANT lurz) — long, branched horns on the heads of members of the deer family

archers (AHR cherz) — people who shoot with a bow and arrow

environment (en VY run ment) — surroundings

game laws (GAYM LAWZ) — a rule to protect fish or animals by saying when, how, and how many may be captured

hides (HYDZ) — animal skins

illegal (eh LEE gul) — not lawful; against the rules

poaching (POCH ing) — hunting or fishing illegally

predator (PRED uh tur) — an animal that hunts another animal for food

prey (PRAY) — an animal taken for food by a hunter

rifle (RY ful) — a gun with a long, thin barrel

target (TAHR git) — something that is aimed or shot at, such as a mark, circle, or object

Most hunting requires tracking the animals.

INDEX

FURTHER READING

Find out more about Outdoor Adventures with these helpful books and information sites:

Schneck, Marcus. *The North American Hunter's Handbook.* Quinlet Publishing/Running Press Book Publishers, 1991.

Internet address for Ducks Unlimited home page (http://www.ducks.org)

Field and Stream Magazine (also found at internet address http://www.fieldandstream.com)